# Darwin's Wild Pursuits Around Downe

Written by
Ewa Prokop

Illustrated by Diana Catchpole

For 'The Truth Behind the Fiction' and more illustrations
visit www.madaboutcharlesdarwin.co.uk

*To those who strive to teach children about British wildlife*

First published 2014 by DB Publishing, an imprint of JMD Media Ltd, Nottingham, United Kingdom.

ISBN 9781780914305

Copyright © Ewa Prokop 2014.

Illustrator: Diana Catchpole (www.dianacatchpoleillustrator.com)

Teachers and parents please visit www.madaboutcharlesdarwin.co.uk

Printed and bound by Copytech (UK) Limited, Peterborough.

# Contents

# INTRODUCTION

Scientist Charles Darwin was born in 1809 in a house called 'The Mount', which is in the town of Shrewsbury, Shropshire. After an education at Edinburgh and Cambridge Universities and a five-year voyage on the H.M.S Beagle, he married Emma Wedgwood in 1839. After living for a period in London, Darwin settled with his family at Down House, Downe, in Kent. He lived there for forty years, until his death in 1882.

Darwin said of himself that he was 'born a naturalist'. He investigated plants, animals and geology in the countryside around Downe. He wrote letters, scientific papers and books about what he discovered. His most famous book was called 'On the Origin of Species'. One of the paragraphs in the book reads: 'It is interesting to contemplate an entangled bank, clothed with many plants of many kinds, with birds singing on the bushes, with various insects flitting about, and with worms crawling through the damp earth, and to reflect that these elaborately constructed forms, so different from each other, and dependent on each other in so complex a manner, have all been produced by laws acting around us .... and that, whilst this planet has gone cycling on according to the fixed law of gravity, from so simple a beginning endless forms most beautiful and most wonderful have been, and are being, evolved.'

The following stories will give you some idea of the places Darwin explored, the species he observed and the investigations he undertook. These days, his 'outdoor laboratory' is very much the same as it was in his day. It is there for you to explore too!

# DARWIN & THE FOX

After luncheon, Darwin put on his coat, took his walking stick out of the cupboard and opened the back door. "Are you coming with me?" he asked his Spitz dog.

"Woof," replied the dog, who got up and trotted through the back door, looking behind him to see if Darwin was following. They made their way past the lawns and hothouse and through the gap in the hedge to Great Pucklands Meadow. They walked down the bank to 'The Terrace' . The dog ran ahead, heading southward along the path towards Cudham Lodge Woods, or 'The Big Woods' as the Darwin family called them.

Darwin and his dog walked between the trees of the Big Woods and under some of the low-hanging branches. Darwin walked stealthily as he had done in the forests of Brazil, in case he encountered any wildlife. They entered a woodland glade where primroses grew. Curled up at the edge of the glade was a sleeping fox. Its head was tucked into its tail and it was quite oblivious to the intruders who had entered its territory. Its orange-brown coat rose gently up and down as it lay snoring. "You know, that I've met foxes trotting home at dawn when I've been up here before?" Darwin said to his dog. His dog replied with a "Ruff" to acknowledge his master's comments. This roused the sleeping fox, who stared at the pair and ran off. Darwin laughed at how his dog didn't feel at all inclined to chase after it.

"Now let's look and see what we've got here," Darwin said. He knelt down on the slope and carefully peeled back one of the lemon-coloured petals of a primrose. "Oh here is one of the pin-eyed types of primrose, with the stigma above the stamens," he announced. Darwin carried on looking amongst the carpet of primroses around him and declared, "Here are some of the thrum-eyed types of primrose, with the stigma below the stamens." His dog wasn't listening though; he had wandered into the woodland sniffing for vole tracks and other scents. Darwin, however, sensed that he was being listened to and watched.

He called out, "Who is there? Declare yourself!" Out from between the bushes came the fox they had previously disturbed.

"It is me, Sir. My name is Vulpes. You know foxes are inquisitive, Sir. I am curious as to what you find so fascinating about these common plants."

"They may be common, but they are exceptional," Darwin replied. "I have been looking at the different forms of flowers and have found that in primroses there are two different forms. I believe this helps the flowers to avoid self-pollination and encourages pollen from other plants of the species to be received. It is the insects which help to exchange pollen between the different forms of the plants."

"But to what advantage?" Vulpes enquired.

"Exactly my question," Darwin remarked." It makes me think that somehow the seeds of a plant that have originated from two different parents may some-how give the offspring an advantage. Perhaps they are better fitted to their environment. Why else have two forms of the same species?"

"You know that cowslips grow here too?" Vulpes enquired.

"Do they? Please show me where they grow."

Darwin followed Vulpes through a part of the Big Woods he had not explored before. Ahead of him, in another glade, Darwin saw the bright yellow flowers of the cowslips.

"Do you know, Vulpes, that some people think that primroses suddenly turn into cowslips?" Darwin announced.

"That's just silly. I know this patch of cowslip plants like the back of my paw. These cowslip plants have always grown here in their present form for as long as I can remember."

"I am growing primroses and cowslips in my garden under different conditions to see if I can witness any transmission of character," Darwin declared, "and if you are correct, the plants will not change with time."

Darwin could hear his dog barking furiously in the distance, seeking some sort of response from his master.

"I'd better go before my dog gets too nervous," Darwin said, "Thank you for your guidance. Perhaps we'll meet another day."

"I'm sure we will," Vulpes replied.

Darwin turned away and started retracing his steps, guided by the barks of his dog. His dog came running up to greet Darwin, jumping up and down with delight that his master was back.

"We best stick together," Darwin said reassuringly as they made their way up to the path heading home.

# DARWIN & THE FIELD MOUSE

It was a warm summer's day. Darwin walked out onto the veranda and shut his eyes, facing the sun as though basking on a beach somewhere. He stroked Phisty, the cat, who was curled up on the wicker chair.

"Today is the day, Phisty, when I undertake my red clover experiment!" Phisty opened one eye, as though to acknowledge what his master had said, and promptly closed it to go back to dreaming about mice.

Darwin walked back indoors to pick up the squares of muslin that he had already prepared. They lay in a leather pouch on the side table. He also took with him a reel of thread and a pair of scissors. "It's going to be a long day," he told himself. He strode out towards Great House Meadow. The oxeye daisies and sorrel were standing to attention in the still air. The red clover plants were growing close to the ground, with the pompoms of florets positioned prominently.

Some of the florets of the red clovers were already open. Darwin avoided these and carefully walked round, identifying those flower-heads that had not quite yet opened. He proceeded to cover each of these flower-heads with a piece of muslin, which he tied in place with a short length of thread. Darwin counted silently in his head as he moved from one area of grassland to another, repeating the procedure. He wiped the sweat that was coming from his brow, took out the flask of water he had been keeping in his pocket and drank a few sips. He watched the bumble bees visiting the various plants in the meadow, including the red clover plants that he had left exposed. Darwin continued with his task into the afternoon.

"There. That makes a hundred. That should be enough," he thought to himself.

A field mouse sitting by a large flint had been watching Darwin's exploits. He licked his lips, having just come from a bees' nest where he had eaten some grubs and honey. Darwin went indoors to cool down and wrote notes of his afternoon labours in one of his little notebooks.

Some six weeks later, Darwin took another excursion to the field on yet another hot day. This time he took with him two muslin bags. He walked around the field and collected 100 uncovered clover heads to place into one of the bags. In the other he placed the cut flower heads of those plants he had covered in muslin. The field mouse sat by the large flint watching Darwin, as he had done before. This time he could not keep his thoughts to himself,

"Sir, what on Earth have you been doing all these weeks? Do you not think it rather a mad pursuit?" Darwin smiled and crouched down to where the voice had come from. "Good day, field mouse. Mad? I think not. I am simply carrying out an experiment. I plan to prove that the bumble bee is critical for the survival of red clover."

"In what way, Sir?"

"Well I believe that bumble bees, rather than any other bees, are the only insects with long enough tongues to reach the nectar in the flowers and therefore the only ones with the ability to pollinate the flowers. If this is the case, then it can be surmised that if for any reason bumble bees became extinct or very rare in England, then red clover would become very rare or wholly disappear."

"Yes, but bumble bees will never become extinct," the field mouse replied firmly.

"Well, say there was a population explosion of field mice in this field, then perhaps you field mice would eat all the combs and grubs of the bumble bees and there would be none to pollinate the flowers."

The field mouse pondered. "True. I see your point. But there will never be a population explosion of mice in this field. The owls and buzzards and foxes and cats – the list goes on – all keep a check on my friends and keep our numbers under control."

"So, don't you see, Sir, it is therefore quite credible that the presence of a feline animal in large numbers in a district might determine, through the intervention first of mice and then of bees, the frequency of the flowers in the district?"

The field mouse pondered further. "I understand. But how are these hats of muslin helping you?"

"The muslin has prevented bees from pollinating the plants and therefore I suspect that no seeds will have developed. In those flowers without muslin, the bees will have been able to visit and pollinate them, therefore I suspect that many seeds will have developed in these plants."

"So ....showing that bumblebees are important to the development of seed in red clover!" The field mouse concluded, nodding his head.

"Exactly!" Darwin replied. "I will go further, Sir. If bumblebees were to become rare, it might be an advantage to the red clover to have a shorter tube to its flower so that the hive-bee could visit. Thus I can understand how a flower and a bee might slowly become, either simultaneously or one after the other, modified and adapted in the most perfect manner to one another to ensure the preservation of individuals."

The field mouse was not convinced. "You mean a plant could change its structure to suit another pollinator?"

"Yes," replied Darwin, "but over many generations."

The field mouse started to think that Darwin had succumbed to heat stroke and that he had started to talk jibberish. "I think it's time you went indoors, Sir. The sun is rather hot today."

"Thank you for your care and attention, Sir. I'll heed your advice. I bid you good day."

The field mouse disappeared between the stalks of grass and Darwin returned to the house. After taking a cool drink, Darwin sat at his study desk and with a set of tweezers started to count the seeds from the pollinated flowers. Leonard ran in and asked "Can you read me a story, Papa?"

"Oh dear, you'll make me lose count! I'll come and read to you in half an hour," Darwin replied.

An hour passed and Darwin exclaimed "2700!" He then took the other bag with the muslin-covered flowers. It wasn't long before he could see that not a single one of the flower-heads had produced any seed.

"Papa. You promised!" came a call from the dining room.

"I'm coming!" Darwin shouted, smiling to himself that his experiment had been worthwhile.

# DARWIN & THE LIZARD

One sunny day Darwin, on his horse Tommy, trotted up the hill on the Westerham Road. He took the path along the edge of Keston Common, past the old gravel pits and the suite of ponds which had been created some years before below the source of the River Ravensbourne. He crossed over the road and followed a track to a little, shallow valley where the peaty soil was saturated with water. The damselflies and dragonflies undertook their acrobatic displays around Darwin and the midges did what they do best and bit him! But this didn't bother Darwin as this was a place where special plants grew. Many different types of bog moss as well as bog asphodel, bog cotton, purple moor-grass and bell heather surrounded him. But, Darwin had not come to see them. He had come to collect a plant which lay close to the soil surface, bearing spoon-shaped leaves covered in sticky red hairs – the sensitive, round-leaved sundew.

Darwin dismounted and took the leather saddle bag off Tommy's back. Out from one of its pockets, he took a magnifying glass, a small trowel and a medium-sized paper box. He knelt down on the ground, oblivious to the water that was slowly seeping through the legs of his trousers, and parted the grass and plants ahead of him. "There you are! Splendid", he said as he congratulated himself in finding some sundew plants at his first stopping point. He took the magnifying glass and peered through its lens to take a closer look at the insects that had been caught by this insectivorous plant. He was astonished to find that even a dragonfly had become entrapped in the hairs of one of the plants. "Just amazing!" he said to himself as he marveled at the nature in which the plant captured its prey. He took the trowel and pushed it accurately into the ground to prize out a number of specimens which grew around him, arranging them carefully in the box. After taking a moment to enjoy the heathland and scattering of trees that encircled the bog, Darwin climbed back onto his horse and headed south, on a slightly different route home, across the main part of the heathland.

As he passed by some gorse bushes, some children came running and squealing from behind them and Tommy was spooked. It took some time to calm Tommy down. "Bother!" Darwin said as he saw his sundews spilt on the ground. "I must have not buckled the bag well enough." He dismounted and started picking up the plants from amongst the heather.

"What are they?" came a remark from amongst the heather plants. Darwin was surprised and curious to know who had posed the question. He looked around him but could not see any animals.

"I'm here, Sir." Darwin bent his head close to the ground to where the voice had come from to find a lizard. It was much camouflaged amongst the leaf litter and stony, sandy soil.

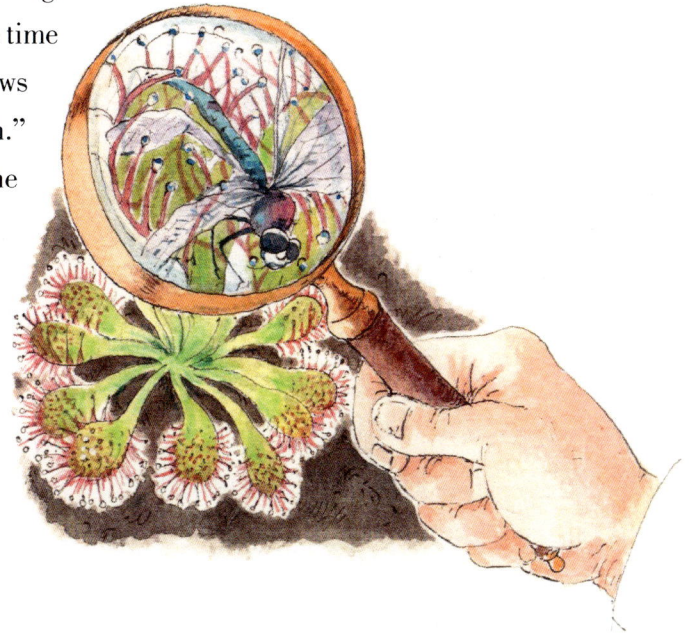

"Good afternoon, Sir," she repeated, "My name is Lacerta, and who may I be addressing?"

"My name is Mr. Charles Darwin, Madam."

"Pray tell, what are these curious plants, Mr. Darwin," the lizard asked.

"They are called sundews because they have hairs that spread out like the rays of the sun. These hairs produce shiny beads of glue, that look like dew. And you are right, Lacerta, they are curious. I am investigating the range of nutrients they require for productive growth and have some notion that they may take sustenance from the insects that come to be entrapped on their hairs."

"A meat-eating plant?" Lacerta giggled.

"Yes, I know it sounds strange but I think this would give this plant some advantage in the poor soil of the peat. I'm testing their reaction to raw meat, roast meat, milk, urine, egg albumen, pollen and gelatine. I have found that the species does not react to starch, sugar, olive oil, cotton thread, dilute alcohol and infusions of tea. I think that this is because these are not nitrogenous substances. It is tempting to test them against many types of chemical, but I fear that there is not enough time in the day to do everything. I do however, intend to test the plants with salts of ammonia and organic acids. Oh, forgive me, I am getting quite carried away!" Darwin remembered about the spilt contents of his box. "Pardon me, Lacerta, but I must guard the roots of these sundews from the sun and return the Drosera plants to the cool of my bag,"

"Please do not apologise, Sir. A scientist must do what he must do," replied Lacerta.

Lacerta emerged a little more from beneath the vegetation to warm herself in the sunshine. Her scaly skin shimmered and the bulge in her abdomen was prominent. Darwin could not help but notice.

"Oh, Madam, I see you have little ones growing inside you."

"Yes Sir, they are safely inside me for the time-being so that I can take them with me to where the sun shines in order to promote their development."

"When are you due?"

"Not long now. A few days," she answered proudly.

"You've given me an opportunity to make an enquiry. Would you happen to know if there are any sand lizards in the vicinity?"

"Yes Sir! No Sir!"

"You mean that there aren't any here?" Darwin asked, for clarification.

"That's right; the soil is not sandy enough. I hear that the nearest ones are by the Kent coast and towards the east in Surrey, but not here."

"Oh, I didn't think so, but I thought I'd ask."

"They lay eggs you know" Lacerta said informatively.

"Yes, I know. I came across one carrying eggs, as a young man. It's just I have a theory."

"Another one?!" Lacerta exclaimed.

"Yes. Ever since travelling on the H.M.S Beagle voyage, I have wondered how islands become colonised with creatures and I sus-pect, in the case of most lizards, that their eggs may be tolerant of sea water."

"You mean that they might float from one land mass to another?"

"Exactly that! But I need to get hold of some eggs to test this out. You see

I have an aquarium at home in which I can store items in salty water for as long as I need to. I had almost decided to write to readers of 'The Chronicle' to ask for their assistance with this matter, and now you have made my mind up that I will."

"Yes, I suppose the leathery shells will survive a trip in a postal bag, if they can survive a journey across the wide sea!" remarked Lacerta.

Darwin got ready to depart.

"Will you be back here?" Lacerta asked.

"Yes, I have no doubt about that. I have been studying the earthworms lying on the grassy and heathery path and why they occur more in one place than another. And then there's the sundew."

"I've noticed that there have been many more visitors here in the last few years," the lizard said.

"Yes, I believe it is a favourite place for those from London wanting to collect the strange plants that are found here," Darwin commented.

"I hope Keston Common doesn't change too much. I like it here."

"I do too," Darwin agreed.

"Well good day to you Lacerta. Congratulations on your forthcoming expectations."

"Yes, I look forward to introducing my offspring to my home."

"No doubt we'll meet again." Darwin said as he trotted away.

Despite going to Keston Common on many an occasion in the years that followed, Darwin did not meet Lacerta again. His chances of seeing her were somewhat reduced by the fact that on occasions he would send one of his servants to collect specimens of sundew. Darwin continued to test various insectivorous plants with chemicals such as the oils of cloves, caraway and chloroform, ordered from his usual chemist, William Baxter. One day he met a young man at the bog, who turned out to be Baxter's son.

"Well, young man, what are you doing here?" Darwin asked quietly. William got up, quite humbled at seeing Darwin standing there.

"I am collecting some Drosera to reproduce some of your experiments, Mr. Darwin. My father is William Baxter, the pharmaceutical chemist who has been…."

"Oh Sir, you need not explain. I know him well. However, it is gratifying for me to also meet his son."

"Well, I am fond of botany and was attracted by some of the experiments you have been undertaking with Drosera. I am just collecting some in my vasculum so that I can reproduce some of the experiments."

"What will you be doing with the Drosera?" Darwin asked inquisitively.

"I do not intend to feed them flies. I thought that I would try them out on sulphur and poisonous alkanoids. I have found Drosera to absorb sulphur."

"How interesting," Darwin remarked, "for that corroborates my experience. But I envy you your access to that mysterious cupboard you have - full of interesting poisons."

"You may of course send for any that you wish for, Mr. Darwin."

"I know! I know! But I should like to try everything!"

They continued to talk about their examinations of the insectivorous plant for a while until Darwin took a quick look at his pocket watch and announced, "Though I could talk with you on this matter all day, unfortunately I must depart. I bid you success with your investigations, Sir. Do correspond with me, if you so wish."

"Thank you, Mr. Darwin," William replied, as Darwin caught his pony and rode away.

# DARWIN & THE DUCK

It was a warm summer's day. Darwin emerged from his study and wandered into the drawing room.

"Emma, I've decided to visit Holwood this afternoon."

"Shall we all go?" Emma answered, "We could have a picnic!"

"If you wish," Darwin replied.

Emma instructed Mrs. Evans, the cook, to prepare some things to eat from the pantry and Moffatt prepared the horse and carriage.

The family assembled in the hallway. Emma divided the excited party into two groups and shepherded the first group through the front door, towards the carriage. Once aboard, the carriage turned out of the driveway and up past the pond at Downe village.

"Look at the ducks and geese swimming in the pond!" Horace shouted. "Can we feed them?"

"Not now," Emma remarked. "Now remember, Lord Cranworth has given us special permission to visit the grounds at Holwood whenever we wish, but you must all be on your best behaviour."

The carriage proceeded along Downe Road and soon after Holwood House came into view on the top of the hill between the two swathes of woodland. "Oh, it's so lovely!" Emma remarked.

As the carriage approached the junction of Shire Lane and Westerham Road, Darwin announced, "It's alright Moffatt, we'll walk from here."

The carriage stopped and the children tumbled out of it, chattering with delight. The baskets of food were grabbed and Moffatt went back to Down House to fetch the rest of the children. Everyone made their way up the track to Holwood House and walked across to the lawns, from where there was a magnificent view southward over the downland valleys. When the others arrived, everyone settled down to tuck into the cold meat pie and scrumptious currant cake.

Some time later, Darwin left Emma reading and the children racing down the pretty green slope and headed westward through the trees to the cluster of ponds he knew. The pond water was quite still, the reflection only broken by the clusters of duckweed which floated at its surface and the ripples created by a lone mallard duck paddling in the shallows. Darwin crouched by the edge of the pond and watched the duck as it bent its neck down into the water, bringing up a shower of water to dowse its feathers. It then made its way to the edge of the pond and waddled its way onto the bank.

The duck was just about to start preening itself when Darwin shouted, "Wait!"

The duck was startled. "My name is Anas, but who might you be Sir with your abrupt tone!"

Darwin apologised, "I'm so sorry, Anas. My intention was simply to deter you from cleaning off your feathers as I wonder whether I could take a closer look at them."

"What a strange request, Sir. May I ask why?"

"Of course you may. My name is Charles Darwin and I live not too far from the pond in Downe Village."

"Oh yes, I've heard of you Mr. Darwin," Anas nodded.

"Well, I don't know whether you are aware but I've been studying how plants and animals can come to colonise new ponds and islands and I believe you may have one of the answers!"

"Me Sir? I don't think so," Anas remarked. Darwin approached Anas and peered across his wings and tail feathers.

"Yes, as I suspected. Whilst you've been in the pond you've picked up some of the duckweed on your feathers."

"That happens all the time!" Anas replied, "I simply preen them off."

"But do you do that whilst you remain at the pond in which this event occurred or do you sometimes arrive with the duckweed at your new destination?"

"It depends," Anas replied. "Sometimes I make myself presentable beforehand, and sometimes after I land."

"Hurrah!" exclaimed Darwin. "This is what I suspected. When you fly from one place to another, you unknowingly carry with you the instruments of duckweed propogation and as such the new pond you visit becomes stocked with the plant."

Darwin then sat and pondered. "I don't wish to inconvenience you, Anas, but I wonder whether you could do me the most greatest of favours. Would you be willing to fly to the ponds on the estate of my good friend, Sir John Lubbock, remain there for an hour or so and then return here again?"

"That is no task Mr. Darwin. Don't you know that my family have been known to travel hours and fly for hundreds of miles without any failing in their condition?"

"I don't doubt it," Darwin remarked.

"But what is your point?" Anas asked.

"Well, I wish to see if you come back with any passengers."

Anas was puzzled but removed as much of the duckweed as he could from his back in preparation for his journey and commented, "I've got to give the right impression, Mr. Darwin as I don't know who I might meet there."

Darwin requested, "If you don't mind, I'll just take a look at your feet before you go."

"There's nothing wrong with my feet! They are the finest webbed assets in these parts! I inherited them from my father."

Darwin commented, "They do look very powerful indeed and perfectly modified for their role."

"Yes, they're just perfect for the dual purposes of swimming and walking and are hardy enough to stand long periods in cold water."

Anas started to beat his wings and in moments was high up in the sky. "See you soon!" he declared, as his voice faded into the distance on his way to High Elms Estate.

Whilst Darwin waited, he could not help but notice the multitude of flowers on the Horse Chestnut trees, which were particularly abundant on the estate. He was interested to find that the trees had both male and hermaphrodite flowers. The male flowers had already gone over and had released all their pollen. "I must return to see the male flowers next spring," Darwin mumbled to himself. He wandered around looking at the particularly numerous earthworm casts left at the surface of the soil. There were many more than he had seen at Green Hill and other places. He noted how some of the casts had disintegrated with weathering and had spread

across the soil surface. "I wonder whether strong winds might be able to shift these worm casts?" he thought. He had long been considering how the action of earthworms might help modify landscapes.

Before long, Anas was back.

"Hello!" Anas quacked as he surfed back onto the pond. "I'm glad I went. There are lots of female mallards at that pond! I must say that their feathers were the most delightful shades of brown. Maybe I can court one of them and next year have some sons and daughters to be proud of." Darwin smiled.

"Do come over here, Anas, and let me have a look at your feet."

Darwin picked Anas up off the pond and cradled him in the crutch of his arm, holding his feet aloft. Darwin looked closely all around Anas' golden feet and had almost given up hope of finding anything, but then exclaimed "Ah-ha! I've found your passengers, Anas."

"What are they?" the duck asked, starting to get worried.

Stuck to one of Anas' ankles were some tiny pond snails. "Some Lymnea have taken a journey with you, Sir. Snails may be slow-moving in character but here you have proved that nature has found a way in which they can be dispersed great distances. The property of High Elms is only a mile away, but you said yourself that your family can travel many hundreds of miles, so perhaps these snails can survive these great journeys too!"

"I am pleased to have been of some service to you, Mr. Darwin. It's also nice to know I might have some company with me on my long flights, even if that company simply comprises of shelled creatures. Now if you don't mind, Mr. Darwin, I must get back to dabbling. My stomach is rather empty and I must feed before the sun goes down!"

"Of course, Anas.'

Darwin crouched down and placed Anas on the grass so that he could get his balance before returning to the pond.

"Thank you so much for your assistance, I am glad to have made your acquaintance," Darwin said. He parted with a "Cheerio!", but Anas was already too busy catching some mayfly nymphs to return the courtesy.

Quite content with his investigations, Darwin strolled back to join his family.

"You've been a long time!" Emma remarked.

"Just got busy. You know how it is."

"I know," replied Emma, smiling. "Moffatt is meeting us at the bottom of the lane at 4 o'clock on the dot, so we had better make our way down the hill."

The family gathered their things together and walked down to Shire Lane where they were soon greeted by the carriage.

# DARWIN & THE ROMAN SNAIL

Darwin finished that afternoon's scientific discussions with his friend, Sir John Lubbock, and made his way out of the mansion, heading south through the woodland out of High Elms Estate and into Cudham valley. He took a moment to take in the view, from where he could see Cudham village and the shaws that fringed the valley summits.

Darwin kept to the western side of the valley along which he had previously seen mulleins growing. It wasn't long before he came across some white mulleins growing at the side of some scrub. He observed them closely and then continued on his journey. He then came across some great mulleins, as he had expected. He sat down on his cloak, beside them.

"Take care, Sir!" came a voice beside him. Darwin looked down to find the eye stalks of a Roman Snail emerging from under the cloak he had just laid down.

"I'm so sorry, Madam. I didn't see you there."

"Another few inches this way and I would have been a wretch of a snail, Sir!"

The snail carried on eating the ribwort plantain it had been feasting on.

"I don't suppose..." Darwin begun hesitantly "you've seen any hybrid mulleins in this area, have you, Madam?"

"Of course, Sir. There are plenty of them growing in the next field down."

"Can you show me, Madam?"

"Well, I suppose I could, Sir. But if you want to get there today, you had better place me on your shoulder so I can guide you. I am otherwise far too slow to accompany you."

Darwin picked up his cloak and perched the snail on his shoulder.

"What is your name?" Darwin asked. "Pomatia," the snail answered.

"That's a lovely name," Darwin replied.

Darwin trudged down the slope, guided by Pomatia. Before long, Darwin saw a suite of mullein plants ahead of him.

"Here they are!" announced Pomatia. Darwin placed Pomatia down on the ground and started wandering amongst the plants. Each one was different from the next. There were some that were extra hairy, or extra tall, more branched or with a greater number of flowers. Darwin was delighted. He checked each of the plants to see if any had produced seeds, but found no evidence of any seeds. He went round again, counting how many he had observed.

"33 hybrids, Pomatia! There are 33 hybrids in this field and every one of these intermediate forms is absolutely sterile! The varieties make an almost perfect series between the two distinct forms of white mullein and great mullein."

"I told you that there were lots of examples here," called Pomatia from amongst the marjoram.

"I think I may dig out one of these hybrids and plant it in my kitchen garden to see next year if it turns out to be sterile," Darwin announced. He clawed away the mud from around the smallest plant he could find and wrapped its roots in a large handkerchief he found in his pocket. "Thank you so much, Pomatia," he said excitedly.

Darwin sat down next to Pomatia and they chatted for a while. "A Mr. Lonsdale informs me that you Roman snails are susceptible to some degree of permanent attachment. He says that he placed a pair of your species, one of which was weakly, into a small and ill-provided garden. After a short time the strong and healthy individual disappeared, and was traced, by its track of slime, over a wall into an adjoining well-stocked garden. He concluded that it had deserted its sickly mate; but after an absence of twenty-four hours it returned, and apparently communicated the result of its successful exploration, for both then started along the same track and disappeared over the wall."

Pomatia giggled, "That is of no surprise to me! Of course we communicate with each other and help each other out when we can. After all, there is plenty of food to go round!"

Darwin continued to ponder. "I don't suppose, Pomatia, you would consider getting involved in one of my experiments?"

"What does the experiment involve?" Pomatia enquired.

"Well, once you come to hibernate and seal your body against the elements, I wonder whether I might plunge you in sea-water for twenty days. I don't know whether there would be any danger involved."

"There will be no danger," Pomatia responded confidently, "but why undertake such an experiment?"

"Well I have a theory that perhaps organisms that are sufficiently protected can survive a journey across the sea to colonise new land masses. I just need the proof." "I'm sure I can assist," replied Pomatia. "Come back when it is cold. I will be hibernating at the base of that gate post over there."

Darwin glanced over to the field gate to check he had followed her instructions correctly. "Thank you, Pomatia. I will see you in the New Year then, on the other side of hibernation."

"Yes, I'll see you again then," replied Pomatia. Darwin picked up his Verbascum and trudged along the valley bottom. "Oh look at these lovely scarlet pimpernels. Both the red and blue variety!" Darwin declared, forgetting he was no longer with Pomatia. Darwin continued up the slopes onto the triangular field by 'Orchis Bank'. He stepped carefully between the ant hills that had colonised there and then made his way up to the road. It had just started to drizzle. Darwin was keen to make his way home before the rain came down more heavily. He quickened his pace and as soon as he got home, planted the Verbascum in the Kitchen Garden.

"It's time to come in, Dear!" Emma called from the house. Darwin walked briskly to the house where the wood, in the fireplace, was already burning, waiting for his return.

# DARWIN & THE HONEY BEE

One April morning, Darwin picked up some black thread and the small pair of scissors from Emma's embroidery box.

"I'm just popping out to Green Hill," Darwin called to Emma, who was upstairs with the children. He opened the back door, walked past the verandah and down the gravelled path into the 'Kitchen Garden'. He took a quick glance at all the things growing there and made his way through the gap in the holly hedge into 'Great Pucklands Meadow'. He took a moment to take in the view across to the Big Woods. "Charming," he said to himself and walked along the footpath down the steep bank and onto 'The Terrace'. He headed northward along the uneven, flinty ground to the lane and crossed over, making his way through the trees to Green Hill. From the top of the slope he could see the carts going along the dog-leg bends of Milking Lane, past the Coal Post, and onto Leaves Green. The trees on the opposite side of the valley were bright green with new spring growth.

Darwin looked about him. The bright yellow brimstone butterflies were dancing along the bank. The ant hills were casting a shadow against the ground. The branches of the beech trees growing alongside the path, shrouded the edge of the bank. The pathside and bank were covered in hundreds of hairy violets. Their almost oily, deep lilac petals and shiny heart-shaped leaves faced up to the heavens. Darwin had come on a mission. He wandered around the bank looking out meticulously for any insects that had come to collect pollen and nectar from the violets. Bees buzzed around him and he remembered one of his first impressions of Downe - the quite extraordinary humming noise coming from the hive bees visiting the local sainfoin fields.

Darwin then spotted a hive bee sitting on a violet, probing its proboscis into the flower. Darwin waited for it to go and then took the thread and scissors out of his pocket and cut a small piece of thread. He tied the thread around the plant and then looked out for more bee activity. A little further down the slope, he noticed another visitation by a bee and repeated the marking procedure. The bee started buzzing in front of his face and came to sit on Darwin's shoulder.

"Are you following me, Mr. Darwin?"

Darwin was surprised that the bee knew his name. "How do you know my name?" he asked

"I've seen you many a time in the gardens at your house. I live in one of your bee hives. My name is Apis."

"Oohh, that's nice to know. Now I know one of the sources of nectar that creates that delicious honey we all enjoy!"

"Yes, we're all quite proud of our honey you know. There are plenty of flowers in the gardens, woods, meadows and arable fields from which we take our nectar."

"I always marvel at the structure of your honeycombs. You are all so clever to be able to create them. It is a skill that must have developed and been inherited in your species over many generations. It is a dull man who can examine the exquisite structure of a comb, so beautifully adapted to its end, without having some enthusiastic admiration for it."

"Pray tell, Mr. Darwin, what are you doing, marking all the flowers I have visited with thread?"

"Well, it's to help me remember which flowers have been visited by you, as I intend to return later in the season to find out which flowers have developed seeds on account of any you have happened to pollinate."

"We try our best, Sir. When we come to collect the nectar, we try to reward the flower by spreading around some pollen." Darwin laughed.

"I think it may be the other way around. I think the flower rewards you with nectar to encourage you to visit and that you happen to deposit the pollen from other violet flowers."

Apis sniggered. "I see what you mean. Well, whichever way it is, the process serves us both."

"Yes, I think this relationship must have come into existence soon after flowers first adorned this Earth."

"Well at least we do it properly, Sir."

"What do you mean?" Darwin replied.

"Well some of the bumble bees do not pick up the pollen from the anthers of open violet flowers. Some access, or should I say steal, nectar from the flowers before they open, by biting holes in their nectaries."

"Really, Apis? I haven't seen that before."

"Yes, just look out for it, and I'm sure you'll see what I mean, Mr. Darwin." Apis buzzed, "I must be on my way, now. Clouds are starting to appear and it is becoming decidedly chillier."

"Yes, good day to you, Apis," Darwin called.

Darwin continued to mark up some flowers visited by other bees, marking six in all. Walking back to the house, he couldn't

help thinking about what Apis had said about the bumblebees. A couple of weeks later, Darwin visited Hangrove, less than a mile east of Down House. Here dog violets grew. It was a warm day and Darwin sat on the bank and waited. Low and behold, a bee of the Bombus hortorum species soon came buzzing around the violets and Darwin watched it. Darwin saw the bee sucking nectar from a multitude of flowers and biting holes in the nectaries. Darwin marked six with black thread, with a view to returning at a later date to see if any had set seed.

Darwin went back to Green Hill some days later to check on the violet flowers he had first marked. Apis saw him from high above and came flying down to buzz beside him. "How did we do?" Apis asked.

"Well, it looks as though two of the six have set fine pods and some of the others seem to be developing seeds, so I suppose you could say that you've done very well! By the way, I did witness a bumblebee biting the nectaries of some other species of violet not too far from here. I await eagerly to see whether the flowers develop their seed too."

"Glad to know you believe me, Sir," Apis called as he flew away to visit the other plants that were now in flower on the chalk slopes.

Darwin smiled and made his way back along the path, towards home.

# DARWIN & THE BADGER

In the evening, an hour before dusk, Darwin looked out of the window and watched the trees and other plants swaying in the gale that had been developing all that afternoon. "Just my opportunity!" he said to himself as he rushed to the hallway to put on his thick woollen coat and hat.

"I'm just going out to see the bryonies!" Darwin called to Emma. He didn't wait for an answer. The heavy front door slammed shut behind him on account of the draught.

Darwin made his way to the path opposite the house and walked across the field owned by Downe Court Manor, through the thicket of trees and into the next field. There on the left hand side was a magnificent hedge. It was full of hawthorns, black-thorns, field maples, hazels and ash. Many plants climbed across the branches of the trees forming the hedge, including dog rose, bramble, traveller's joy, ivy, honeysuckle, hops, bitter-sweet and black bryony. But Darwin had come to see one particular climbing plant - the white bryony.

Darwin walked slowly along the path beside the hedge, scanning the branches for this climbing plant. He was looking out for the characteristic five-lobed leaves. It was the time of year when both the little green flowers, of the male and female plants, and the reddening berries, of the female plants, were on display. "Ah-hah!" Darwin exclaimed as he saw a plant growing at the bottom of the hedge. He focused on its tendrils. Darwin had already observed at home how these tendrils revolved or spiralled and how they were so sensitive to contact that they rarely ever failed to seize upon thin sticks or blades of grass placed in their path. These tendrils had grasped the stems of a tall cocksfoot and blackberry bush in the plant's struggle to reach the light. Darwin watched the coil stretch out and bunch up together, like a spring, as the wind howled around him. "Perfectly formed! Like a ship with two anchors down," Darwin said to himself. "I knew the tendrils would be able to withstand the most extreme of conditions!"

Darwin continued to walk along the hedge to witness other examples of the plant being tested by the wind. It was getting dark now and he hadn't taken a lantern out with him, so he knew he needed to get back as soon as he could. But then he heard a rustling sound at the bottom of the hedge and the sound of munching. Darwin wondered what it could be and waited in the gloom. Soon, a black and white striped snout appeared carrying a mouthful of earthworms. It took a moment to scratch itself and sniffed the air, wary of the human smell he could sense in the area.

"Let me introduce myself," Darwin said, "I'm Charles Darwin and I live at Down House."

Talking with his mouth full, the badger responded, "Good evening Sir. I am Meles. I live at Green Hill."

"Oh yes, I know it well. I have often passed by the badger sett there and wondered whether I would ever meet its occupants. I am honoured."

Meles blushed. "Apologies that I look a bit of a state. I've just had to battle through this thick hedge."

"On the contrary, Sir, your tough hairy coat has served you well. There is not a hair out of place."

Meles scratched himself again and sucked up the worm he spotted emerging from the worm burrow ahead of him.

"Do you know, Meles, that earthworms have played an important part in the history of the world?"

"In the very least, they have kept my species supplied with food. They're our favourite!" Meles replied.

"Exactly," Darwin remarked, "and they have ploughed the land, protected artifacts, decomposed leaf litter which would otherwise be lying on the surface, provided tunnels through which plant roots can grow.... I could go on!"

"I sense that that is the case!" Meles smirked.

"There are so many of them that ten tons of earth passes through their bodies on each acre of land."

"Yum!" Meles commented.

Darwin observed the low, rounded back, the wide paws, bulky shoulders and the long claws of Meles.

"Is there something wrong?" Meles enquired, now getting quite self-conscious about his appearance.

"Oh no, Sir. I am just admiring your adaptations for digging. Do you know that the form of your species has not changed for many generations. At least as far back as the Pliocene period."

"There is no need for change, Mr. Darwin. Why change something that is perfectly fit for its purpose?"

"Yes, but perhaps at some point your ancestors were different - not as well formed. And it was only those most well adapted that could survive and produce the next generation of badgers, well fitted to their environment. These ancestors have passed on these positive traits."

"All I know," said Meles, "Is that my great grandfather looked similar to me."

"Yes, that will certainly be the case," acknowledged Darwin. "Now, Sir, I must depart as my wife will be worried about where I have got to in the dark."

"Do you need any assistance on your return to Down House?" Meles responded, "I can guide you if you like."

"Yes, that would be most helpful, Meles, not only for the assistance but for your company."

Darwin and Meles chatted away as they carefully made their way back across the fields towards Luxted Road.

"Do help yourself to the worms in Great Pucklands and Great House Meadow," Darwin said.

"Don't worry, I do!" Meles replied cheekily.

Darwin watched Meles waddle away into the dark. Darwin opened the front door and closed it tightly behind him. "I'm home!" he called, and Leonard and Horace came rushing from around the corner to greet him and to find out about the expedition.

# DARWIN & THE NEWT

One August morning, Darwin decided to visit his sister, who was teaching at the school in Cudham. "I'm just going to Cudham School, Emma. I'll be back in the latter part of the afternoon."

"That's fine, Charles. Don't forget we have visitors this evening."

"I won't, Dear," he called as the side door to Down House slammed shut.

Once Tommy, Darwin's trusted horse, had been saddled up, Darwin took mount and trotted out of the driveway, turning right down along Luxted Road. A while later, he turned up Jail Lane towards Biggin Hill. Cudham School soon came into view, its flint walls shimmering in the hot summer sunshine.

Darwin looked at his pocket watch and saw he had arrived rather too early. He dismounted and led Tommy into the fields behind the school, tying him up on an old post and leaving him feeding on the grass. "I won't be long, Tommy," Darwin announced, as he made his way onto the footpath, disappearing amongst the oak and hazel trees into the welcome shade.

Darwin walked on a little and smiled as he saw the light bouncing off the surface of the long-made pond he had already become acquainted with. "You're looking a little dry," he remarked out loud, as he observed the muddy banks and the low water levels on account of the long dry summer which had not afforded any fresh rainfall to this twinkling jewel. A water hen sat at the edge of the pool, underneath the low branches of a holly bush. She observed this unexpected visitor. The cattle and sheep in the surrounding fields, past the thicket of trees that encircled the pond, were, on the other hand, unaware of Darwin's presence.

"Now then, what can we see here?" he said to himself. 'Burreed and broad-leaved pond weed, I think. Then there's brook-lime, spearwort, water plantain, rushes, floating grasses and duckweed, of course!" He double-checked to see that he hadn't missed anything. "Now what about the invertebrates?" he mumbled. He crouched down by the edge of the pond. The mud clung to his boots and Darwin knew he would get a stern look from the footman on his return home. Darwin cupped his hands in the water a few times to see what he could catch and once again started to list what he saw. "Water snails, Cyclas, bugs and beetles!" Darwin patted the notebook in his pocket to remind himself to write down all that he had seen on returning home.

Below the water's surface, a creature was listening in to Darwin's mutterings and was alarmed to have not been spotted. He swam, sinuously, to the edge of the pool, lifted his head up above the water and announced, "I think you've overlooked something!" Darwin's heart took a little leap.

"Sir, you have given me quite a shock!"

"Apologies, Sir. Let me introduce myself. I am Triturus and have lived in this pond for some eight years. How have you come to know of my residence? Have you been here before?"

"Yes, a few years ago, one April. I took some mud from the edge of this very pond and..."

Triturus interrupted, in disbelief, "Why on earth would you do that, Sir? My mother did tell me that a gentleman had done this very thing. That was also the year when she remembered there being 3000 or more frog tadpoles in the pond!"

"Well if I may finish, Sir, I will tell all. I took a sample of mud from underneath some leaves and roots of some water plants and then some from the margin of this pond and parcelled them up to take home. I weighed the mud, which amounted to quarter of a pound. I placed the samples in a container and supplied them with sufficient light conditions and waited. Low and behold, I counted 51 seedlings grow from the damp mud. I was convinced that people were unaware of how charged with seeds mud can be and how seeds may be fitted in a manner highly useful to them for survival once a pond dries out. In fact, you're surrounded by a potential jungle of plants this very moment!"

Triturus looked around him noticing only a handful of plants growing there. "But it is not a jungle now, Sir!"

"That's because the circumstances are not suitable. They will appear when the time is right. Not necessarily all at once of course. And even when they do germinate, they will have to contend with being eaten by beasts of all sizes and may not survive to produce the next generation of seed!"

There was an awkward silence. Triturus didn't know enough about the topic to continue the conversation and seeing that Darwin was an educated man, took this information as perfectly acceptable news.

"Oh, this does bring back memories, Triturus. I remember fishing for newts in an old quarry by my school in Shrewsbury, when I was just 8 ½ years old. They were the same kind of newt as you."

"What do you mean, Sir. Surely there is only one kind of newt?"

"There are in fact three types of newt in England. You may know that you are a type of newt called a smooth newt. Then there is the great warty newt and the webbed newt."

Triturus gasped. His mind was already buzzing from the first revelation, but the second seemed unimaginable. "Why would there be three kinds of newt?" Triturus asked.

"Well that is the beauty of descent with modification!"

"Descent with what?"

"Modification!" Darwin exclaimed. Triturus was now finding it difficult to cope.

"Let me explain," reassured Darwin, "Many thousands of years ago there was probably an ancestor you all shared. But then perhaps three different populations became separated and came to inhabit slightly different areas. As generations came and went, only those individuals with characteristics most adapted to their environment survived to reproduce and slowly these characteristics came to be adopted in a new species.

Do you mind, if I take a closer look at you, Triturus?"

"You may, but I hesitate to ask why."

Darwin scooped Triturus up into his hand. "Look at your back feet. They do not have webs between the toes. However,

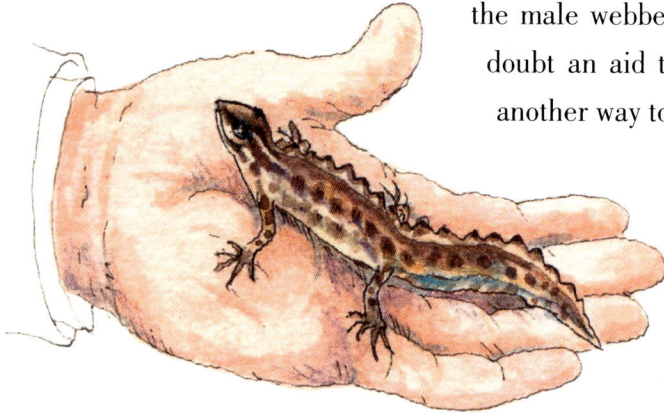

the male webbed newt does have such an adaptation in the spring and this is no doubt an aid to his eager search and pursuit of a female. Your kind has found another way to attract the females."

"You mean my crest?"

"Yes! What is the purpose of this ornament in the breeding season when it does not aid you in locomotion? It must be there to attract a female! And of course, along your stomach you become much more colourful, showing a bright orange belly marked with round dark spots. You must have noticed how this attracts the female kind?! Triturus blushed, "Yes, I suppose so, Sir."

"This characteristic has been passed down many generations, as this is the characteristic that has proved the most successful in courtship. Therefore the characteristics of the three primitive newts to which I have already referred become diverged over time."

"I think I understand now, Sir"

"But of course, Triturus, I have seen other types of newt across the World."

"What's 'the World'? Actually, do not answer that. Please Sir, do not fill my head with any more of your splendid observations. I have started to develop a headache from all the information you have divulged."

Darwin laughed. "I understand, Triturus. It has taken me many years to work this out. I'm thinking of including these facts in one of my books."

"You mean, I'm going to be famous?"

"You could say that!" Darwin chuckled. "I will devote a section of my book on the embryonic development of newts and on the existence of sexual selection in newts."

"That would be fabulous, Sir," Triturus replied.

Darwin suddenly became conscious of the time. "Now I must take leave, as my sister is probably waiting for me and may be rather cross that I've been so long."

"It's been a very eventful day, but before you depart, what is your name, Sir, so that I may address you more favourably next time we meet."

"Just Darwin will do. I must dash. Good day to you, Triturus!"

"Good day!" Triturus bubbled as he sank beneath the water's surface to moisturise his delicate skin.

"Sorry, I've been so long, Tommy". Darwin apologised. Tommy neighed in response. He'd long become used to having to wait patiently for Darwin to complete his investigations.

# DARWIN & THE SQUIRRELS

One late summer's day, Darwin was walking around the 'The Big Woods' near his home as part of his afternoon stroll. He crept slowly across the leaf litter and fallen twigs, to make as little noise as possible. He took position behind a tree to witness a stoat bounding its way across the woodland floor. He stood stock still and watched it for a good ten minutes. He was just about to depart homeward-bound when he felt some creatures clambering up and around his legs. Up in an ash tree close-by, an adult red-squirrel was calling in great distress.

"Come here, children. Come quickly!" Her young squirrels had mistaken Darwin for a tree and were still busy circling around him, giggling as they pursued each other. "Don't worry, Madam. They are quite safe," Darwin announced.

The young squirrels were surprised to hear a voice coming from their 'tree' and ran as fast as they could back towards their mother. Darwin watched them at a distance as they climbed up an oak tree. The acorns were just in their early stages of development. Darwin saw how the squirrels hanged upside-down to retrieve them from the branches. They then sat hunched on a large tree branch, nimbly manipulating the acorns in their paws as they nibbled them. They then took hold of some leaves on which some semi-transparent spherical galls were attached, and prized them off to eat the maggots within. "So they are insectivorous!" Darwin said out loud.

"We eat what we need to eat to survive, Sir!" the mother shouted as she lept across to another tree, with her children following. They soon disappeared into the distance.

Darwin wandered along the valley and up onto the path that led towards 'The Terrace'. The hedged boundary to his field, Great Pucklands Meadow, soon came into view. Here, in springtime, Darwin had observed thirteen spindle trees growing close to one another; some were hermaphrodite and some were female. Now being late summer, the orange seeds were developing within the garish pink fruit, so Darwin inspected the trees to see which had produced the most fruit. It had been a good year; the branches of some were heavily laden. He counted the fruit on each of the trees and saw that the female trees had produced significantly more fruit than the hermaphrodite ones. "This shows their greater fertility," he said to himself. Darwin pondered how perhaps dioecious plants may have an advantage over the hermaphrodite ones. He had already started to think that perhaps, through time, a plant could change from having both female and male parts to having female and male parts on separate plants. The branches along the hedge started to lightly shudder. Darwin glanced up to see the squirrels watching him.

"The female spindles always produce more fruit, year after year!" commented the mother squirrel.

"Thank you for confirming my observations, Madam," Darwin replied.

The squirrels jumped down to the ground and accompanied Darwin as he made his way along the path. After a while Darwin announced,

"I will take a slight diversion, Madam. I wish to see whether the autumn gentians are in flower yet."

Darwin walked down the slope, with the squirrels following on behind. Darwin surveyed the slopes to find some purple gentians growing on the chalky soil. Some of them were the double-form, which Darwin had noted many years earlier. "You see, Madam, the double flowered plants are generally dwarfer than the perfect plants, their leaves are less pointed and the entire plant much less symmetrical. Some people used to think that these double-flowered specimens were created from an excess of food, but I have found them growing on this poor chalk soil."

"They are rather pretty, aren't they Sir?" the mother squirrel proposed.

"Yes, they are. It is good to see them growing here all these years later. Now Madam, may I suggest that you partake in the beech nuts that are growing up on the shaw, there. It is a particularly good year for them."

"Yes, thank you for the advice. We will wander up there and have a feast."

"I have my own feast waiting for me at home," said Darwin. "Tea and scones!"

"Good day!" they called to each other as they went their separate ways.

# DARWIN & THE STAG BEETLES

The Darwin family spent the afternoon with the Bonham-Carters at Ravensbourne Lodge in Keston. Darwin was getting restless at not having met his afternoon routine of going for a walk. "If you would excuse me, ladies and gentleman, I will stretch my legs and take a short stroll in nearby Padmall Wood." Darwin made his way out of the house and walked eastwards.

Darwin entered the wood. The large, serrated leaves of the old sweet chestnut coppice stools dominated his view. The white bark of the silver birch coppice stood out brilliantly in the sunshine, the delicate leaves dancing in the light summer breeze. Darwin noted in his mind the presence of aspen, alder, crack willow, rowan, holly and hazel trees. The bracken fronds waved as they picked up the air currents and the pink cones of rosebay willowherb flowers swayed from side to side. The honeysuckle was in full fragrance around him and the purple-flowered ground ivy below him dispersed its fragrant oils as it was crushed beneath his feet. He passed by a coppice coupe which had been cleared the previous winter by the forester of Rookery Estates. Many of the side branches arising from the forestry work had been left on the woodland floor and were now beginning to decay. Plants, such as tormentil and foxgloves, were growing between them.

Darwin approached an old stack of timber at the edge of the coupe. Much of it was already rotten and bark had flaked onto the woodland floor. He started to peel away some bark and lift up some old logs on the look out for any beetles he could find. All that emerged was a slow-worm. Darwin then heard a rattling noise coming from behind a birch tree. He slowly made his way to the birch tree and peered past it. Ahead of him he could see two male stag beetles pushing against each other, clashing their 'antlers', in a quest to win the prize of courting the female stag beetles in the wood. Darwin could not control his excitement at seeing the pair and exclaimed, "How wonderful!"

The stag beetles stopped what they were doing and turned round to see who they had impressed.

"Oh, I'm so sorry, Sirs. I didn't mean to interrupt your dual," Darwin said, quite embarrassed. The beetles climbed up the tree beside which they had been fighting, their antennae moving relentlessly with curiosity at the man who had so readily revealed his delight at their meeting.

"It's just that I haven't seen many stag beetles in my time and never before have I seen two males, fighting. It's quite fascinating," Darwin explained.

"That is our purpose, Sir," the two beetles said in tandem.

One continued, "We have been living underground for a good seven years and…"

"Speak for yourself, Sir," the other beetle said, "I have been underground for five years only, feeding on the rotting timber that has been left here."

"And," interrupted the other beetle, "We only have a few weeks in which to find females with which to mate. As males, we must compete for the best areas in which females reside. I have just flown in from Hayes."

"And I have just flown in from Farnborough," reported the other beetle.

"Have you seen any females?" the two stag beetles enquired of Darwin.

"Not yet," said Darwin.

"So we're in time!" they said in unison.

One continued, "The females emerge from their pupae a little after the males and we have a good suspicion that there will be some emerging from the very wood pile you were inspecting."

"Well," said Darwin, "I will always have a fascination in beetles. As a student I used to go beetle-hunting at every opportunity and shared my interest with my cousin, Fox. On one occasion, in fear of losing three of the beetles I had caught, I remember popping one in my mouth, only to have to spit it out again as it released some unpleasant chemical. I can even envisage the very spots I came across certain beetles, though many years have passed. I remember collecting many beetles when on my travels around South America too."

"You mean you captured and killed them?" the beetles said together, looking nervously at each other.

"Yes, but I don't do that anymore."

The beetles breathed a sigh of relief.

"Do you mind if I continue to watch you sparring?" Darwin said.

"By all means, Sir."

The beetles took up their positions on the tree and it wasn't long before one fell to the ground with a thump.

"Hoorah!" shouted the victorious beetle.

The loser, crawled slowly to another tree – a rowan – and climbed up its trunk. It launched itself off, expanding its wings from beneath its wing cases and hovered off towards the direction of Bromley Common.

"Now, I'll just sit and wait," said the victorious beetle.

"I'll take my leave, Sir. I must be getting back to my hosts."

Darwin waved goodbye to the stag beetle and made his way back through the wood along the River Ravensbourne, where the water mint, common figwort, marsh thistles and purple loosestrife were in bloom.

On return to Ravensbourne Lodge, Darwin shared his delight at seeing the insects with his hosts. "I have just seen some wonderful stag beetles!" Darwin announced to the crowd. The gathering listened eagerly to Darwin's encounter. Darwin also explained how one of his naturalist colleagues, Mr. Davies, had once enclosed two male stag beetles with one female in a box. The larger male severely pinched the smaller one, until he resigned his pretensions. He also explained to his avid listeners how a friend, when a boy, would often put males together to see them fight and how he had noticed that they were much bolder and fiercer than the females. The males would seize hold of his finger, if held in front, but not so the females. The afternoon went by in a flash.

# DARWIN & THE BUTTERFLY

Darwin made his way across the fields, south of Downe Court Farm, and down the footpath to Cudham Road. In his hand, he carried a butterfly net. He walked along the lane to Hangrove cottages and walked down the footpath onto Orchis Bank, one of his favourite places. Darwin surveyed the view. He could see the spire of Cudham Church to the south and the trees of High Elms Estate to the north.

The sun was shining. The insects were flitting about and the birds were singing in the bushes. The wildflowers were in all their glory on the narrow stretch of chalk grassland which lay between two strips of woodland at the site. Darwin admired the yellow rock roses, the blue milkworts and the white eyebrights carpeting the grassland sward. But he had come to see the orchids. He wandered around the slope hoping to discover all those he had seen before. Over the years he had found the bee orchid, man orchid, fragrant orchid, common-spotted orchid, common twayblade, musk orchid, greater-butterfly orchid, birds-nest orchid, fly orchid and broad-leaved helleborine. This time, the most common orchid he encountered was the pyramidal orchid. These were at their peak, in full flower.

Suddenly, Darwin whisked the net from under his armpit and across the pyramidal orchids growing closest to him and looked through the meshwork of his butterfly net. He could see an orange butterfly staring back at him.

"Sir!" the butterfly proclaimed, annoyed, "You merely needed to ask me if you wanted a closer look at me. Why reduce me to such primitive a means of capture?"

"So sorry, Sir, but I couldn't take the risk of you flying off before I could inspect your head," Darwin replied.

The butterfly started to wriggle. Darwin put his hand into the net. The butterfly clambered up onto Darwin's index finger and clung on tight as Darwin lifted him out of the net. Darwin brought the butterfly up to his eye level and stared intently at the butterfly's face. The proboscis was covered in pairs of orchid pollinia.

"You are a large skipper butterfly aren't you? I haven't written you down yet!"

"You are right, Sir. But what do you mean by 'not having written me down'?"

"Sorry, I should of course explain. My son George, I and some naturalists I know, have been trying to find out which insects pollinate the pyramidal orchid. You know - the flower you just visited? So far we have found there to be seventeen moths and five butterflies. You are now our sixth butterfly species."

"Which other butterflies visit this orchid?" the butterfly asked.

"The common blue, small copper, marbled white, small skipper and grizzled skipper."

"Yes, I am familiar with all these species. They all live in this area. And it makes sense that you have only accounted moths and butterflies as we are the only ones with a long enough proboscis to reach into the elongated nectary of the pyramidal orchid. The scent is so sweet, I cannot help being attracted to it. But it is a bother that these pollinia structures become attached to me whenever I do so."

"Oh, Sir, these structures are fascinating. Rather than form loose pollen, the orchids produce these club-like structures with coherent masses of pollen. These are designed to attach to any insect that comes to sip the flower's nectar. When you go to visit another pyramidal orchid, do you not find that some of these structures become displaced?"

"Yes, I have noticed that," replied the butterfly.

"Well, in this way the orchid ensures that its pollen gets transferred to another plant of its kind. It thus ensures fertilization and the development of future seed! I doubt whether there is anything more beautiful."

The butterfly was surprised at how enthused his capturer was about the whole process.

Darwin continued "Do you know that within a mile of my house grow thirteen different types of orchid! So all around me these exceptionally modified plants are being visited by a host of insects with which they have developed a special relationship. I'm going to write a book about it all." Darwin paused. "You may be interested to know that I am growing a comet orchid in my greenhouse which has an extremely elongated nectary , almost twelve inches long! I predict that one day someone will find an insect with a proboscis just as long as this, showing that they have mutually adapted over a long period of time."

The butterfly sensed that Darwin could talk the whole afternoon about orchids. "May I have your permission to be on my way, Sir?" the butterfly enquired.

"Oh yes, Sir. Sorry to keep you. Thank you for your time." Darwin responded apologetically.

"With pleasure, Sir," the butterfly said as it gently beat its wings and fluttered off northward towards the other chalk grasslands in the valley.

# DARWIN & THE RABBIT

Darwin walked across the fields near Downe Court Manor and along the lane to Hangrove. He made his way down the slippery slope which cut across 'Orchis Bank' and dipped over the ancient woodland bank below it. He stopped to admire the white helleborine orchids that he knew would be growing there. Darwin then heard something rustling at the base of a hazel coppice stool nearby. He looked over to try to make out what it was. A shrew lifted its head up from beneath the old fallen leaves, glanced at Darwin, and hurried off. But Darwin had already noticed something else. Growing at the base of the stool was a strange, pink plant, destitute of true leaves and breaking through the ground in the form of an arch. Darwin took his pocket knife out of his coat and started to dig around the base of the plant. He saw that the strange plant had subterranean scale-like leaves and its roots were closely associated with the roots of the hazel. "This must be the toothwort!" Darwin advised himself. As there were a number of these plants growing in the vicinity Darwin took his knife and cut through the stem. Out from the cut seeped some sappy fluid, just as a tree sapling exudes sap if cut in spring. "The parasitic roots must be absorbing water and this is how the plant pushes its way through the soil!" Darwin proposed to himself.

Out from the corner of his eye he saw the twitching nose of a rabbit that was watching him. Seeing that she had been spotted, in a moment the rabbit was off across the valley. Its pale feet and white tail could be seen flashing with every step it made into the distance. Darwin was now distracted. He placed the toothwort and knife in his pocket and started walking along the path which cut across the valley bottom and up the steep bank towards Lordfield Shaw. Just before he reached the yew and beech trees, he veered off to the right, where there was a fantastic view across the valley and a series of rabbit burrows dug into the bank. By now, the rabbit had easily reached its burrow and was standing on its hind feet at the burrow entrance waiting to see what Darwin would do next. Darwin laid out his coat on the ground and sat down. The rabbit was puzzled. She had expected him to be pointing a shotgun by now. She whispered to her kits, who were bunched up below the entrance to the burrow, "Stay low." The rabbit now went down on all fours, her ears rotating to listen in to any noises that were coming from Darwin's direction. Darwin continued to watch her.

"Have courage, Cuniculus," the rabbit murmured to herself. She slowly bounded off towards Darwin and sat a good twelve feet from him before announcing "What can I do for you, Sir?"

"'Nothing, Madam. I am just observing your habits." Darwin replied.

"My habits, Sir? Why, I'm observing your behaviour, Sir. The absence of a shotgun, for instance."

"I'm not here to find my next supper, Madam. I am merely here to find out some information about you. May I ask, do you and your family exercise a lot and are you sufficiently supplied with vegetation for your sustenance?"

"Of course, Sir. We run around whilst playing and whilst running away from foxes, stoats, birds of prey and men! There is also plenty to eat on this grassland and within the woodland," Cuniculus replied.

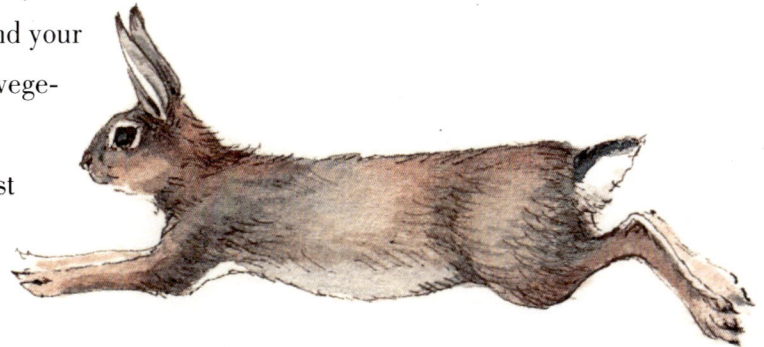

"May I ask whether any of your friends and family, are, how shall I put it, on the larger side?"

"We are all slim and fit, Sir."

"Have you ever come across domesticated rabbits?" Darwin enquired.

"What Sir, you mean rabbits that have come to live with humans? I've never heard of such an unlikely story!"

Darwin smiled. "Well, let me tell you Madam, that mankind breeds many different types of rabbit. All different colours. Some with lopped ears. Some very heavy in weight."

"I've never heard such nonsense," Cuniculus shrilled.

"Yes, it's true Madam. They are given very nutritious food and have little exercise. As a result, over many generations, the shape and weight of their bones – in their limbs and skulls - has altered. The thickness of their fur has also diminished and…"

"Stop, Sir. I do not wish to hear any more about it. There is only one type of rabbit and yes sometimes we have aberrations in our colonies producing different colours, but to say that we can be altered to such an extent is ludicrous. I'm sure we could all still breed with each other. There is just one species," she professed.

"I don't doubt it," Darwin agreed, "I'm sure these unusual breeds came from an ancient ancestor that was tamed."

Now feeling safe, Cuniculus started to graze the grasses and wildflowers surrounding her.

Darwin saw an opportunity and asked "I don't suppose…." Darwin paused mid-sentence, realising that his next request might be too much for the rabbit to bear.

"Finish your sentence, Sir. I haven't got all day to talk about silly things."

Darwin continued, "I don't suppose you know of a rabbit skeleton in these fields I could take for examination?"

"You amaze me, Sir, with your bluntness. We don't talk about the dead you know." Cuniculus took a moment to ponder. She didn't wish to get even more agitated at Darwin, after all, it would be unladylike.

"We don't talk of it anymore, but there is an abandoned warren at the bottom of the slope. You are sure to find some remains there as a fox caught one of our own there a few months ago. The body is bound to have decomposed by now and a skeleton now evident."

"Thank you Madam. You have been most kind. I will leave you to your day."

Darwin got up and tread carefully down the hill, avoiding the numerous rabbit holes. He came to the warren the rabbit had mentioned and crouched down beside it. Amongst the turf that had grown up around one of the main entrances was a rabbit skull. He looked carefully for more pieces of the skeleton but none could be found. He placed the skull in his pocket and looked back to see that the rabbit was now running around with her kits on the slopes. Darwin marched across the valley and up onto the lane to make his way home. When he got home to his study, he bathed the skull in water, dried it and labelled it 'Downe', ready to be analysed on another day.

# DARWIN & THE WREN

Darwin headed out across Great House Meadow, behind Down House, past the old ash trees and towards the lane. He crossed over the lane and headed across the arable fields, through the gap in the hedgerows and into the beech wood that lined Cudham Road. There he paused to look at the wood anemones, white stellaria and brilliantly blue bluebells. There was one other plant that struck his attention too - the white-flowered wood sorrel.

Darwin looked at the wood sorrel at the edge of the woodland where there was full sun, and at others which grew further into the woodland, where there was less light. As expected, the leaflets were in different positions. "So well adapted to the diffuse light of the woodland floor," Darwin affirmed to himself. Darwin was well aware that the leaflets of this plant opened and closed like a parasol with the intensity of the sun. He had been informed by Professor Batalin, the previous year, that the plants would shrivel and die within a few days, if the leaflets were prevented from depressing when exposed to intense sunshine.

Darwin made his way to the meadow between Hangrove Hill Wood and Twenty Acre Shaw. He noted how the chalk-loving plants were starting to develop their flower buds. He sat on a large fallen trunk just below a big beech tree and waited to see what wildlife he could spot. He did not have to wait long before seeing some deer pass down the middle of the hatch and out towards the fields below Cudham. He listened to the characteristic calls of the long-tailed tits making their way from tree to tree along the edge of the woodland. He noticed some black ground beetles and some ladybirds scuttling along the ground by his feet. Beside him was a thicket of low brash, bramble and briar. He noticed a wren fly out from it and decided to take a closer look at the place from which it had emerged. He parted the vegetation. Inside, he found a domed cup of moss, leaves and dead grass, lined with feathers. Nestled within the construction were three white eggs marked at one end with brown speckles. Darwin smiled and replaced the vegetation.

"Ouch," he squealed as one of the rose thorns pierced his finger tip.

"Serves you right, Sir!" came the alarm call of the wren which had now returned. "Do you not know that it is important to keep the eggs camouflaged from predators at all times. I cannot afford for a magpie to see you rummaging around in my carefully constructed nest, you know!"

Darwin was not used to being scolded. "I'm so sorry, Madam. I was just taking a peek."

"A peek is all it takes Sir! A peek is all it takes!"

The wren flew back into the nest and rocked side to side until she was comfortably settled on her eggs. Darwin felt he needed to compliment the wren on her perfectly coloured feathers. "Your feathers, Madam, are well suited to your brooding duties. If I hadn't seen you fly out, I would never have known you were there. Your brown feathers so complement the browns and greens of the vegetation around you."

"Thank you Sir. I accept your observations. Now good day to you. Please leave me to my duties."

Darwin tipped his flat, wide-brimmed hat to say good-bye and wandered back into the wood.

As Darwin emerged onto the path, he saw a boy reaching up to a birds nest that had been made in the branches of some young saplings. The boy could not quite reach. The boy, not having noticed Darwin's arrival, took a gasp when he turned round to see a tall, grey-bearded gentleman standing there in a black cloak and hat.

"Good day to you, Sir.'

"Good day to you, young man. I see you are looking for birds nests."

"That's right, Sir."

"You and I share an interest then. Indeed I find it difficult to understand why every man should not be an ornithologist. Would you like me to show you the nest of a wren?"

"Yes, please do Sir. I have never managed to find one before."

Darwin led the boy to where the wren was nesting. Darwin coughed to announce his arrival. "Madam, may this boy see your suite of beautiful eggs for a moment?" The wren was chuffed at receiving another compliment. "If you must. But be quick about it!"

She flew onto a nearby branch and watched the young boy look into her nest. His hand started to reach out into the nest and the wren sent out an alarm call and bobbed up and down, with her tail feathers erect.

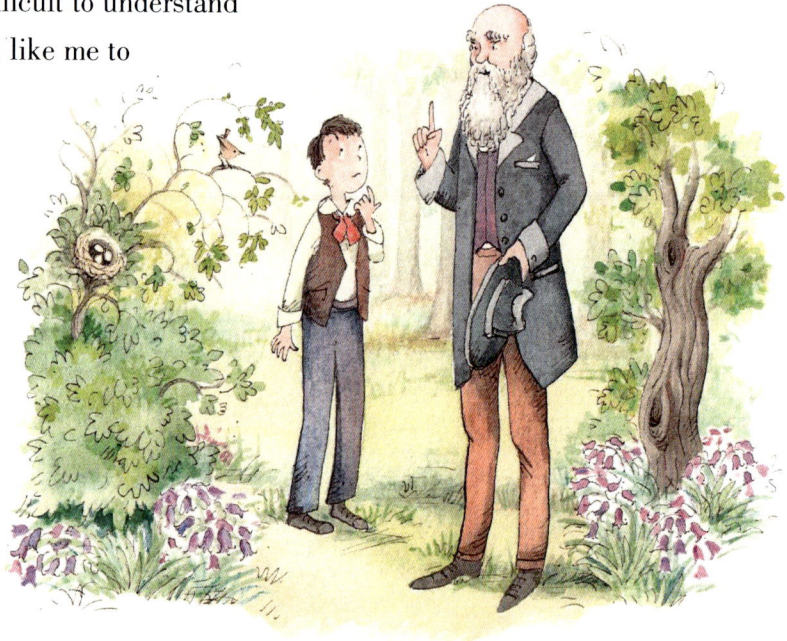

"Stop, boy! What do you think you are doing?" Darwin said abruptly.

"I just wanted to take one of them home."

"Absolutely not! Don't you see how big a challenge it is for a bird to lay this amount of eggs? How much of themselves they have invested in their offspring?!"

"I hadn't thought about it, Sir" the boy replied.

The two ornithologists moved away from the nest to let the wren resettle herself. Darwin continued, "I used to be the same as you in my youth. I used to collect eggs and pierce them and dislodge their contents so as to store them in a collection, but I see now that it is just wrong. Please change your ways and simply observe the beauty of the eggs you find."

The boy was embarrassed, "I will, Sir."

The boy turned down through the woodland to make his way back to Cudham village, whilst Darwin turned up towards the fields, homeward bound. When the boy got home and reported what had happened to his father, his father laughed. "You have just met the famous Mr. Darwin! He probably knows more about birds eggs than any other person living." The boy smiled from ear to ear.

# DARWIN & THE SPIDER

One autumn evening, Darwin lay on the sofa whilst Emma played Beethoven and other pieces on the piano. Darwin admitted to her, in one of her breaks in playing "If I had my life to live over again, I would have made a rule to read some poetry and listen to some music at least once a week."

"I know, dear, but in this life you have had much else to do," she replied comfortingly. Darwin opened the door to the veranda and settled in a chair outside to watch the setting of the sunset. He clutched the blanket that lay around his shoulders in an effort to shield himself from the chill in the air.

As Darwin watched the view, his eyes were drawn to a spider that came into view in the near distance. It had just sent out a web-line so as to drop down from the web it had constructed in the ironwork of the veranda ceiling. It suspended in front of him.

"Lovely music," the spider said, "Is that your wife, playing?"

"Yes Madam. She plays very well," Darwin proclaimed. "May I ask your name?"

"Of course, Sir. It is Araneus."

"Males of your kind produce music in the season of courtship, don't they?" Darwin asked.

"Yes. The sounds are quite charming, much as the tender musical tones of this piano. We don't like music to be too loud, you know."

Darwin smiled. His friend, Romanes had already discovered in his investigations that spiders did not like the loud-playing of orchestras very much.

They listened together to the end of the Mozart piece being played. Darwin then continued the conversation, "I very much admire the specialist web-secreting apparatus you house in your bodies. The fact that you can spin such amazing webs and make your way across spaces by throwing out web-lines is fascinating."

"Yes, we spiders like to think of ourselves as quite unique," she replied, puffing up her body with a sense of pride. "But may I make the point that emerged young spiders at first spin an irregular web and only gradually learn to make a larger and finer one so that practice and experience play a great part".

"Fascinating!" said Darwin. "But I have heard, Madam, that crippled spiders that can no longer spin a web to trap prey can change their habit to become hunters." "That's right," replied Araneus, "Unfortunately, it happened to my sister when she got two of her legs trapped under a stone. She had to live under the ivy over there and scuttle out whenever she encountered a potential morsel of food passing by."

"It is fascinating that an animal can have two very different instincts under different circumstances, isn't it?" Darwin divulged, "but I also hear that changes in habit can occur at different times of life in spiders too. I have heard that some hunting spiders when they have eggs and young, give up hunting and begin to spin a web to catch their prey."

"Yes its funny, isn't it?" replied the spider, "All these different instincts we are born with!"

"Returning to the matter of your web, Madam. I have a friend who has discovered that when he touches a support of a web, the spider at the centre of the web turns to face the vibration. That it senses the vibration through its feet along the radial threads of the web. If it is not in the centre of the web or already on the thread that is being vibrated, it must first go to the centre of the web."

"That's absolutely correct!" the spider said, 'but we never leave the centre of the web without a thread along which to travel back."

"Yes, he has noticed that too," Darwin replied. "My friend says that the instinct of constructing nets for the capture of prey occurs in no other class of animals and is often done to an extraordinary degree of perfection. He says that the nearest he can find to web-spinning in other creatures is for locomotion or cocoon-spinning, as in caterpillars. He agrees with me that web-spinning is a rare faculty and must have had its earliest origin very far back in the history of the class of spiders."

The spider suddenly disappeared, making her way back up to her web. The web was vibrating because a moth had been caught upon it. Darwin looked up. Just as Araneus was to sieze the moth and deliver poison through her piercing fangs, a bat flew past and grabbed the moth with its hind feet. "Bother!" said the spider.

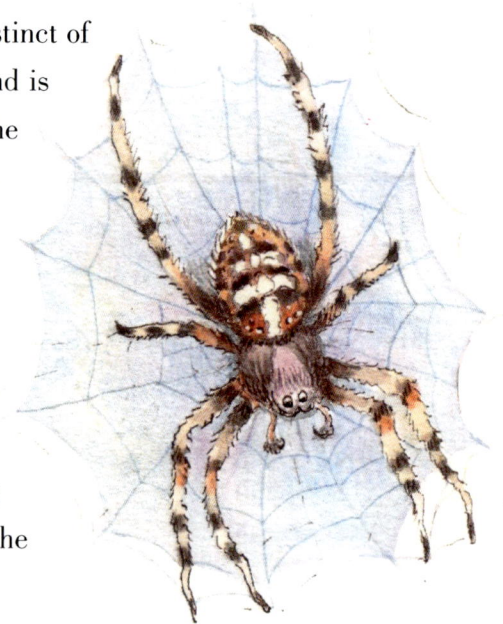

The spider made her way back down to speak to Darwin. "I'm going to have to make a new web. A bat stole my evening meal and in the process damaged my masterpiece, but I think I'll wait until the morning to restore my trap."

"Sorry to hear that, Madam. But you must admit that bats are quite fascinating. Did you know that their wing membranes extend from the top of the shoulder to the tail and that their framework of bones is the same as in the hand of a man! This shows the gradual modifications of similar parts of the body in different species."

"That may well be the case, Sir, but what audacity to test its modifications against mine!"

"Of course, Madam, I do agree that it was an unacceptable act."

They sat in awkward silence for a few minutes. Darwin then offered, "If it is not too presumptuous of me Madam, I will make the effort to squat a few flies tomorrow and place them in your web so that you do not feel you have lost out on a day's provision."

"That would be a most kind gesture, Sir," the spider replied.

The sun had now long set. Emma called to Darwin, "Do get indoors, Charles. There is a distinct draft in the room and you must be chilled to the bone by now." Darwin then became conscious of the temperature and shivered. "I best bid you goodnight, Madam, and take a hot drink. I will see you tomorrow."

"Yes, good night, Sir, and sweet dreams," the spider replied affectionately.

Araneus made her way up to the corner of the verandah roof and Darwin got up to make his way into the drawing room. Emma had a cup of tea waiting for him and soon after they went to bed.